Suzuki

CELLO SCHOOL

Volume 8
Cello Part
International Edition

AMPV: 1.01

Copyright © 2018, 2016, 2003, 1991, 1982 International Suzuki Association
Sole publisher for the entire world except Japan:
Summy-Birchard, Inc.
Exclusive print rights administered by Alfred Music
All rights reserved.   Printed in USA.

Available in the following formats: Book (0361S), Book & CD Kit (40754), and CD (0945)

Book	Book & CD Kit
ISBN-10: 0-7579-2486-7	ISBN-10: 1-4706-3478-3
ISBN-13: 978-0-7579-2486-6	ISBN-13: 978-1-4706-3478-0

INTRODUCTION

FOR THE STUDENT: This material is part of the worldwide Suzuki Method® of teaching. The companion recording should be used along with this publication. A piano accompaniment book is also available for this material.

FOR THE TEACHER: In order to be an effective Suzuki teacher, ongoing education is encouraged. Each regional Suzuki association provides teacher development for its membership via conferences, institutes, short-term and long-term programs. In order to remain current, you are encouraged to become a member of your regional Suzuki association, and, if not already included, the International Suzuki Association.

FOR THE PARENT: Credentials are essential for any Suzuki teacher you choose. We recommend you ask your teacher for his or her credentials, especially those related to training in the Suzuki Method®. The Suzuki Method® experience should foster a positive relationship among the teacher, parent and child. Choosing the right teacher is of utmost importance.

To obtain more information about the Suzuki Association in your region, please contact:

International Suzuki Association
www.internationalsuzuki.org

Under the guidance of Dr. Suzuki since 1978, the editing of the Suzuki Cello School is a continuing cooperative effort of the Cello Committees from Talent Education Japan, the European Suzuki Association, and the Suzuki Association of the Americas.

CONTENTS

NOTE: The ISA Cello Committee recommends that the entire Suite No. 1 in G Major by J. S. Bach be taught before the student completes book 8.

Editing is at the discretion of the teacher.

*Piano accompaniments begin on track 8.

**Piece 4 includes both fast and slow accompaniment tracks, 13 and 14 respectively.

Sonata in G major

Giovanni Battista Sammartini
(1698-1775)

4

This page has been left blank to facilitate page turns

Allegro Appassionato

Op. 43

Camille Saint-Saëns
(1835-1921)

*Alternate bowing

Élégie
Op. 24

Gabriel Fauré
(1845-1924)

Scherzo
Op. 12

Daniel van Goens
(1904-1930)